An American Treasure
The Hudson River Valley

photographs by Ted Spiegel

text by Jeffrey Simpson

Sleepy Hollow Press

Library of Congress Cataloging-in-Publication Data

Spiegel, Ted.
      An American treasure.

      Bibliography: p.
      Includes index.
      1. Hudson River Valley (N.Y. and N.J.)—
Description and travel—Guide-books.   2. Hudson
River Valley (N.Y. and N.J.)—Description and
travel—Views.   3. Hudson River Valley (N.Y. and
N.J.)—History.   I. Simpson, Jeffrey.   II. Title.
F127.H8S74   1986   974.7'3   86-13062
ISBN 0-912882-70-0
ISBN 0-912882-62-X (pbk.)

First Printing.

For information, address the publisher:

      Sleepy Hollow Press
      Sleepy Hollow Restorations
      150 White Plains Road
      Tarrytown, New York 10591.

Manufactured in the United States of America.

Contents

From a tiny pool near Lake Tear of the Clouds, high in the Adirondacks, to the towers and canyons of New York City, the Hudson River Valley has become a symbol of the hopes and aspirations of a nation; in the harbor, the Statue of Liberty is an everlasting expression of freedom. *(Preceding pages.)*

Overlooking a Hudson River landscape unchanged since Henry Hudson first explored the River in 1609, the Cloisters *(above)*, at Manhattan's northern end, shelter a medieval art collection under the auspices of the Metropolitan Museum of Art.

Introduction

The Hudson River, one of the great rivers in the history of the world and the human imagination, is an anomaly in many ways. It is, for one thing, not very old at all as rivers go. A mere twelve thousand years ago, a minute in geological time, as the last glacier of the ice age melted, a river which flowed from the north into a freshwater lake to the west of the Palisades broke through boundaries of rock and debris into the Hudson's present day channel. For another thing, the River is not particularly long. Compared to the Nile's 4,000 miles, the Missouri-Mississippi's 3,988, and even the Rhine's 820, the Hudson's 315 miles seems to be a modest length at most. And finally, one might almost say that the Hudson begins at its end in terms of the attention it gets and in terms of human history. This, of course, is because of the wonderful culmination of the River in New York Harbor, a saltwater arena with more than 500 miles of navigable waterfront, which Robert Boyle, Hudson River bard and conservationist, calls quite simply "the finest natural port in the world."

In fact, the River has a complex life throughout its length, and its upper reaches are the source of many important ideas which make up our sense of ourselves as a nation. The Hudson River Valley is the home of the United States Military Academy, at West Point, training ground for the nation's officer corps since 1802; a partnership between Robert Fulton and Robert R. Livingston resulted in the steamboat *Clermont*; Vassar College, one of the first women's colleges in the world, has been at Poughkeepsie since 1861; Saratoga Springs set the tone for the nation's resorts all through the nineteenth century; and possibly the most significant movement in nineteenth-century American painting was called "The Hudson River School."

Most of the historical events and institutions of note are located in what we could call the "Hudson River Valley proper"—the 150 miles from Albany south. In the slightly greater distance north to the River's source in Lake Tear of the Clouds, high in the Adirondacks, there is a variety of landscape ranging from peaceful water meadows to the heights and depths of the wildest mountain scenery. Purists will say that these northern reaches are not "The Valley," and, geographically speaking, they are correct. But in a river as short as the Hudson and as rich and diverse in geography, history, and beauty, no mile of it is to be ignored. The Hudson River, its valley, its mountains—the Adirondacks, the Catskills, the Ramapos, the Shawangunks, and the Taconics—its mansions, and its legends are where much of America comes from and the place to which—in a day or two's drive—we can go home again.

Chapter I
The Harbor

It is the harbor which we hear about first in the European experience of the Hudson River Valley, and the harbor which, vitalized by the presence of New York City and graced by the Statue of Liberty, demands our introductory attention to the Hudson.

Giovanni da Verrazano, a Florentine exploring the North American coast for the King of France in 1524, was probably the first European to see New York Harbor. He wrote to the King that his ship, the *Dauphin,* had found "a pleasant place below steep little hills, and from those hills a mighty deep-mouthed river ran into the sea...." Next, in 1609, Henry Hudson, an Englishman exploring for the Dutch East India Company and burdened with a contentious crew in a ship called the *Half-Moon,* sailed into the harbor and pronounced the hills around "as pleasant a land as one can tread upon." Robert Juet, who kept the log of the *Half-Moon,* recorded something which other early Europeans were to remark on, namely the strong, fresh smells coming from the water and vegetation, smells which to European noses accustomed to crowded, squalid cities signalled the promise of the New World as surely as the abundance of game and fish.

Once Dutch Nieuw Amsterdam (New York after the English conquest of 1664) was established in the harbor, the worth of a magnificent port which had a river at its back, navigable for 150 miles into the interior, was proven again and again. It was not until the early-nineteenth century, however, with the completion of the Erie Canal linking the Hudson to the Great Lakes and the establishment of regularly scheduled shipping lines between New York and Europe, that the harbor became the most busy and successful in America.

Then, on May 21, 1871, a French sculptor named Frédéric Auguste Bartholdi, who longed for the opportunity to create a monumental piece of sculpture which would uphold the image of French glory (and, it must be admitted, his own glory also), sailed into New York's busy harbor and found both the location and the subject for his creation. As he later wrote, "when one awakens in the midst of that interior sea covered with vessels which swarm like a crowd in a public square...I myself felt...it is certainly here that my statue must rise; here where people get their first view of the New World, and where liberty casts her rays on both worlds."

Bartholdi's statue, known at the time of its unveiling on October 28, 1886, as "Liberty Enlightening the World," and ever since as simply the Statue of Liberty, was an immediate success. It expressed the mythic image that New York Harbor and its source—the Hudson—had come to have in American life.

The biggest city in the richest country in the world, the technological marvel of modern civilization, New York with its skyscraping buildings, its skyscraping opportunities and dreams—as well as the gritty realities of life—for millions of people has embodied, at least since Bartholdi's day, the opportunities of America. The crowded harbor, which was celebrated by more than Bartholdi (Henry James called it full of "restless freedom"), was the landing point for millions of immigrants between 1870 and 1950. And the Statue of Liberty, crafted according to a unique design by Gustave Eiffel which allowed the copper skin to expand and contract on a steel frame, was a physical expression of the type of technology—as well as the eternal hopes—for which New York has become known.

In 1986, heralding its centennial, the statue was unveiled again, cleansed of one hundred years of wear and tear and grime. Rusting internal ribs were replaced, new rivets were put in, seams and holes were caulked with long term sealants, the statue's uplifted arm (which was placed incorrectly in 1886) was shifted a bit and an entirely new torch of copper and gleaming gold plate was lighted. Although it has kept the rich green patina of a century, the statue greets its more than 2 million visitors per year strengthened and made fresh.

Over the centuries of use and the last hundred years of industrial development, the harbor itself had become badly polluted. Nonetheless, controls have been effected, public concern has been aroused for several decades, and the harbor tides are now somewhat cleaner than they were, while upstream, beaches on which raw sewage lay in the 1960s are now clean enough to use. Just as the Statue of Liberty has served as a symbol of America and New York's best aspirations for a century, so now its refurbishing can be seen as the token and harbinger of a pledge to return the harbor and the River to a fresh vitality.

The waters around Manhattan bustle with activity: against the mid-town skyline, cruise ships load their passengers *(opposite page)* while tugs wait to guide them to sea; a sailboat race in the Hudson passes the Empire State Building *(above)*.

Some of the more easily recognized landmarks of New York City are associated with the Hudson River. A jazz combo *(above)* entertains passengers on the Staten Island Ferry; the George Washington Bridge, a marvel of technology when built in 1931, joins New York's famous skyline to create a brilliant light show *(opposite page)*.

Chapter II
Sleepy Hollow Country

The River's remarkable depth in its passage from the interior allowed the Dutch to establish a settlement near Albany—which they called Fort Orange—before they were settled on Manhattan Island. The principal interest of the Dutch in the Hudson Valley for much of the seventeenth century was fur. Beaver, otter, mink, and muskrat filled the holds of Dutch ships returning to Holland, and filled the coffers of the Dutch West India Company which sponsored settlement of the colony.

Because the great interest of the Company was in trade, settlement was only encouraged as it contributed to trade. The attempt was made by the Dutch West India Company (the trading group which represented government in the colony) to put the burden of settlement on individuals who were encouraged to buy land from the Indians—up to sixteen miles along one shore of the River or eight on each shore. These people would be called *Patroons* and they were to be given the rights of feudal lords over the tenants whom they were required to establish on the land. Several patroonships were founded, although Rensellaerswyck (which included Albany), was the only one to survive. The property of an Amsterdam jeweler who never even saw his domain, Rensellaerswyck was home to his descendants until well into the twentieth century.

After the English conquest of the colony in 1664, however, a system of manors was established. Frederick Philipse, who had begun his career as a carpenter under Governor Peter Stuyvesant, in 1693 was declared lord of the Manor of Philipsburg, covering approximately 52,500 acres of today's southwest Westchester County. Stephanus Van Cortlandt, the first native-born mayor of New York City, bought parcels of land in northern Westchester County until his 86,123 acres were chartered by Royal Patent in 1697 as the Manor of Cortlandt.

Some manors continued as economic and governing units until the 1840s, and in many ways helped shape the nature of the settlement of the valley—with a whole continent offering its riches, many immigrants did not choose to become rent paying tenants while open land beckoned. The pastoral culture of the thinly settled valley held sway through the nineteenth century with agriculture, lumbering, fur trapping, and small industries such as brick and cement making and ice cutting, serving as ways to make a living.

The unpretentious but abundant life of the great manors, on which dozens of people worked around the manor house, has been restored at Van Cortlandt Manor in Croton-on-Hudson and Philipsburg Manor, Upper Mills in North Tarrytown. Sleepy Hollow Restorations maintains both, as well as Sunnyside, the home of Washington Irving, who immortalized Valley legends. Philipsburg Manor is the oldest, and in its rough stone manor house, its dam, gristmill, wharf and granary restored to the working conditions of the early 1700s, the frontier life of those rough days is vividly realized. The mill was expanded after

1702 (when Adolph Philipse inherited the estate from his father Frederick) and there are millstones for grinding wheat and corn. In the eighteenth century the mill was so successful that flour and sea biscuits were even exported to Europe; today a resident miller not only feeds corn into the hopper, but is also a master trained in the old style who tends his equipment in such ways as cutting grooves into the stones—a process which is called "dressing the stones."

Van Cortlandt Manor, inhabited by that family until 1945, has been restored to its appearance in the late-eighteenth century and represents another stage of the civilizing process in the Valley. Van Cortlandt Manor had less commercial activity than Philipsburg Manor, although an inn was maintained (and has been restored) several hundred feet away from the mansion. The Ferry House, as it was called, is on the Croton River where travelers taking the ferry could spend the night before they continued their journey on the Albany Post Road. The Manor House itself is of stone and clapboard with a steeply pitched roof sheltering a second story veranda which is approached by a double stairway. In the slender-posted elegance of the veranda and the sweep of the sheltering roof, the house suggests a Southern plantation house which functionally, as the center of a large agricultural estate, it resembled. Inside, the mansion's furnishings are representative of a sixty-five year period, so that Queen Anne and Chippendale magnificence keep company with more austere lines of Federal days. There are touches of local color, such as the Delft tiles depicting Biblical scenes around the fireplace, and generally the ambience of the house recalls the early years of the new American nation.

Sunnyside, where Washington Irving lived between 1835 and 1859, is the single most potent symbol in the Valley of what the old Dutch heritage came to mean in the nineteenth-century American imagination. Irving, who was influenced in his writing by Sir Walter Scott's romantic use of Scottish legends, created enduring literature from the yarns and customs which early settlers had generated about the Hudson Valley. The Hudson River skippers sailing up to Albany and back, through the calms of the Tappan Zee and the twisting channels beneath the wooded hills of the Highlands, invented and remembered legends to account for the boisterous thunderstorms and the sometimes threatening Indians. Robert Boyle in *The Hudson River* quotes the theory of historian M.W. Goodwin that when the Dutch emigrated from their small, flat, cultivated country to the wild corrugations of the Hudson Valley, "the sense of wonder from this change in their accustomed surroundings...peopled the dim depths of the *hinterland* with shapes of elf and goblin, of demons and superhuman presences." Many of the immigrants who arrived in the eighteenth century under the British were Germans from the Rhine Valley, and a relationship can be traced between legends such as Rip Van Winkle's long sleep and old German folk tales. Irving took the tales he had read as a young man and in whimsical, gentle caricature gave the Hudson a native past. With "The Legend of Sleepy Hollow" and "Rip Van Winkle," Irving transformed immigrant experiences into American fables.

Sunnyside had been a tenant farmer's cottage on the Philipsburg Manor, and Irving turned it into a fantasy of an old Dutch cottage. He added stepped gables and antique weathervanes and described the result as "a little, old-fashioned stone mansion all made up of gabled ends, and as full of angles and corners as an old cocked hat." The house today is much as Irving knew it, with all its charm restored. A wisteria vine cloaks the doorway, while inside Irving's study is still furnished with the couch where Irving would nap of an afternoon and the massive desk which was a gift from G.P. Putnam, his publisher.

Lyndhurst, just a half-mile north of Sunnyside, is a near contemporary. It is a grand Gothic mansion, which takes Sunnyside's fanciful adaptation of the past many steps further. Now owned by the National Trust for Historic Preservation, Lyndhurst was designed in 1838 by Alexander Jackson Davis, who virtually created the Gothic Revival Style in America. Gothic Revival was partly a reaction to the severity of the classic revival pillars and white clapboards which had been defining early nineteenth-century American architecture, and partly a celebration of the nineteenth-century Romantic's fascination with the distant past. Lyndhurst, which has been named by Gothic Revival scholar Jane Davies as both "the beginning and culmination of Hudson River Gothic," was built for General William Paulding, a one-time mayor of New York, and enlarged by architect Davis for George Merritt, who bought it in 1864. From 1880 until 1964 the mansion was owned by members of the family of Jay Gould, railroad magnate and financier. Lyndhurst's architect was an intimate of Thomas Cole and the Hudson River School of painters who also created a landscape vision of nineteenth-century Romanticism in the Hudson Valley.

In its thrusting gothic points and turrets of Sing Sing marble, as well as in the source of the fortunes which built and maintained it, Lyndhurst could not be more unlike low-spread mansions such as Van Cortlandt Manor, hugging the land from which they drew their existence. By the time Lyndhurst was built, the Erie Canal—and shortly afterwards the railroads—connected the Hudson River Valley to all of America, and the money which supported the newly built great houses was no more local farming wealth than were the houses themselves overgrown farmhouses. In the few miles between Lyndhurst and Van Cortlandt Manor two centuries of Hudson River life are covered and at least two completely different states of American mind—from the Philipsburg manor house, which served immigrant pioneers, it is a distance of worlds as well as centuries to Lyndhurst, which celebrates the civilized romance of the River in its proud towers built by the might of industry and trade.

Well before the days of Gothic towers on the Hudson and for some time afterwards, the principal means of transporting freight, livestock and passengers between New York and Albany was the all-purpose Hudson River sloop. This broad-bottomed, dependable vessel was built in the style of Dutch canal boats with a vertical stern, a broad bow, and a single mast, well forward. The bottom was comparatively flat with an adjustable center-board (first developed on these boats), so that if the sloop ran aground it could rest harmlessly until the tide floated it off. Sailing on the Hudson was not terribly hazardous in those days, but the progress was erratic. Tides in the Hudson sometimes run with a difference of an hour or more between one bank and the other, and the winds can roar with devastating suddenness through the Highlands mountains. There were record sails of fifty miles in five hours, while other times the same distance took as many days to accomplish. Still, as late as the 1890s when they were finally edged out by steam-powered tugs and barges, sloops were carrying an enormously profitable volume of brick, stone, dairy products, livestock and wheat between the upper Hudson and New York City.

Since 1969 the sloop *Clearwater*, reincarnated from those old days but far from ghostly, has carried a message of environmental awareness up and down the River and through the polluted waters of the harbor and Long Island Sound. The *Clearwater* was born of an idea held by folksinger Pete Seeger, who today is one of 8,000 members of the Clearwater organization. The *Clearwater*'s regular crew of six and its rotating crew of volunteers—including Pete Seeger—take school classes, conservation groups, and officers of industries located on the River for excursions during which they talk about the River's history and trawl for life on the river bottom. Steve Stanne, environmental educator for the organization, has said, "Our nets haul up the expected beer cans, but we also get flounder, porgy, blackfish, blue crab, and once in a while a sturgeon. We try to show people that the Hudson is alive in spite of all the abuse it's taken."

With the end of the Livingston-Fulton monopoly, steam-powered River travel became largely the province of the Day Line, which operated boats between New York and Albany from the late-nineteenth century until the *Alexander Hamilton* made its last trip in 1971. The Day Line has been revived as a round trip excursion, sailing in the summertime from New York to Poughkeepsie and back, but there are no more stern or side wheelers. The *Alexander Hamilton* was the last in American coastal waters. In 1925, the Day Line's best year, over 100,000 passengers travelled between New York and Albany; now, although the Dayliners go less than half the distance and stop only at Bear Mountain State Park and West Point, it is still a fine way to see the majesty of the Palisades and the splendor of the Highlands. For excursion enthusiasts who want to view Manhattan from the much published but almost inaccessible vantage point of the River, the Circle Line Cruises, which travel around the island in a three-hour tour from April to November, offer information and the vista of one of the greatest wonders of the contemporary world: the Manhattan river facades and skyline. Hudson River writer Tim Mulligan quotes Henry James who wrote in 1905 in the *American Scene*: "The sordid city has the honour, after all, of sitting there at the Beautiful Gate." Mr. Mulligan lauds James's sense that the River dignifies the city, but the might of Manhattan viewed from a Circle Line boat surely suggests that the honor is conferred equally both ways.

Onshore, there are excellent routes for meandering day trip excursions by car. From Rockland and Westchester counties, immediately north of New York City on the River's west and east banks, one can travel the entire length of the Hudson River Valley on quiet country roads and slow-paced state highways. "Shunpiking" rewards the traveller by presenting opportunities to experience the Valley's natural wonders, and splendid villages and towns, spontaneously.

The Palisades—a great wall of rock, columnar in appearance—rise from the River's west bank in New Jersey and run for nearly fifty miles north into Rockland County. The early settlers named the cliffs "palisades" because the vertical ridges in the rockface seemed to them like the palisades or wall of standing tree trunks which was erected to protect a fort or settlement; to the Indians the cliffs were known as "weehawken," meaning rows of trees. Preservation of the Palisades began in 1900 with the formation of independent commissions in New Jersey and New York states. Protected since 1937 by the combined Palisades Interstate Park Commission, the Palisades offer miles of wilderness area and biking and climbing trails, as well as the Palisades Parkway, a road which is beautiful as well as efficient.

On the River's west bank, Nyack is a river town filled with Victorian architecture and more than seventy antique and craft shops. Westchester County on the east bank, known for its affluent suburbs, is also home to nineteenth-century villages such as Bedford, where a courthouse from 1787 and a schoolhouse from 1829 are established as museums in a town filled with Greek Revival architecture, much of it "museum quality" in itself.

Farther up the river, the *Commander* is an excursion boat which leaves the West Point dock and cruises south to the Bear Mountain bridge or north into the Highlands. The West Point dock was the embarkation point for faculty, visitors and cadets all through the nineteenth century. From here Col. Sylvanus Thayer, "the father of West Point," stepped onto a downriver boat one June evening in 1833 and sailed away, never to see his beloved academy again. From here, in 1861, brother cadets took boats which would land them in their Northern and Southern homes on opposite sides of the nation's bloodiest war ever. As the *Commander* steams away from the gray stone battlements and ramparts of West Point, onto the bosom of the River, one has a sense of how central to the American spirit and to American history the Hudson Valley has been.

The Dutch first explored and developed the Hudson River Valley. In more recent times, modern-day tourists from Holland have taken Zuider Zee sloops across the Atlantic on freighters, then enjoyed the Hudson Highlands Dutch-style *(left)*. The Philipsburg Manor upper kitchen *(below)* reflects the simplicity of colonial America.

The world of the great Hudson River Valley manors has been restored at Philipsburg Manor, a colonial-era agricultural and trading complex in North Tarrytown. Operated by Sleepy Hollow Restorations, Philipsburg Manor today is the scene of an annual spring festival, Pinkster *(above)*; inside the gristmill *(opposite page, top)* the miller "dresses" or cuts grooves into the millstones using traditional tools. Inspired by the peaceful Philipsburg Manor landscape *(opposite page, bottom)*, a painter captures the timelessness of the site on canvas.

In the slender-posted elegance of its veranda and the sweep of its steeply pitched roof, Van Cortlandt Manor *(overleaf, top)* resembles a Southern plantation house. Hyacinths, tulips and apple blossoms border the "Long Walk" *(overleaf, right)*, which runs from the manor house to the Ferry House inn several hundred feet away; a wisteria vine *(second overleaf, left)* blooms above the manor house stairway, adding to the rich spring colors found at Van Cortlandt Manor.

Sleepy Hollow Restorations' authentic historic landscapes utilize varieties of bulbs, perennials, and herbs—many rarely grown elsewhere today—that were introduced into the region before 1814 *(overleaf, details)*.

Daffodils liven the hillside above Washington Irving's home, Sunnyside *(above)*; later, apple blossoms and tulips *(left)* announce the arrival of warmer weather. During the Christmas season, Sunnyside's dining room *(far left)* is decorated as though Irving might come through the door at any moment.

Less than a mile apart, in Tarrytown, Lyndhurst *(overleaf, right)*—once the Gothic-style home of Jay Gould—and Sunnyside *(overleaf, left)*—near the Tappan Zee Bridge—exemplify the rich variety in Hudson Valley architecture.

27

A reconstruction of an old Hudson River sloop, the *Clearwater (opposite page)* has for two decades carried its message of environmental awareness—and celebration— up and down the Hudson. Folk singer Pete Seeger *(left)* and the 8,000 members of the Clearwater Association have devoted their energies to preserving the River's resources and its timeless landscapes. Piermont Marsh *(below)*, on the west side of the Tappan Zee, provides a luxurious medium on which the River's abundant aquatic life can feed.

The Palisades *(opposite page)*, which run beside the River on the west bank from Weehawken, New Jersey to the Highlands, and Haverstraw Bay *(above)*— only twenty miles from New York City—exhibit the verdant richness of the Valley. In the Haverstraw Marina *(left)*, swans float nearby—but elegantly aloof from—the pleasure craft moored there; undoubtedly intended to grace ponds on the many large estates in the area, these swans bear mute testimony to the diversity of wildlife which inhabits the River's banks.

The Hudson River can have a significant salt content as far north as Newburgh, sixty miles above Manhattan's Battery Park, and ocean fish which swim upriver to spawn have traditionally formed some of its best catches. Men fishing for shad in the shadow of the Tappan Zee Bridge *(overleaf)* will catch one of the most delicious fish swimming in American waters; sturgeon, once so plentiful in the River that they were known as "Albany beef," in recent years have made a comeback in the Hudson *(inset)*.

The Hudson River Valley
has long been a source of
inspiration to both amateur
and professional artists. Near
Haverstraw Bay, a local artist
(above) renders the scene in
applique embroidery. One
reason for the perennial
fascination of artists with
Hudson River subjects may
be the variety of the native
flora; the sight of an *opuntia
leptocarpa (right)* is an
unexpected pleasure of
the Valley.

36

Throughout the Hudson River Valley, residents may take for granted a level of artistic and cultural life usually available only in the big city. In Westchester County, the Caramoor Music Festival *(above)*, held each summer in the Venetian Theater, has gained Caramoor an international reputation. Located in Katonah, Caramoor is a Mediterranean-style estate built originally by a New York lawyer to house his collection of European and Chinese art.

Nearby, the stained glass windows, created by Marc Chagall, which grace the Union Church of Pocantico Hills *(overleaf)* represent the only cycle of church windows created by the modern master in the United States. Members of the Rockefeller family commissioned these windows, as well as the final work completed by Henri Matisse before his death, which appears above the altar. Although the Union Church is an active congregation, the beauty and peacefulness of the church can now be enjoyed by the public through tours given by Sleepy Hollow Restorations.

A quiet afternoon drive or bicycle ride can lead to delightful surprises in the small towns of the Hudson River Valley. The Old Dutch Church and the adjoining cemetery *(opposite page, left)*, across a busy highway from Philipsburg Manor in North Tarrytown, provided the setting for Washington Irving's immortal tale, "The Legend of Sleepy Hollow." Settled over three centuries ago, Bedford Village *(opposite page, right)* contains stunning examples of Greek Revival architecture within a community which has retained its rural identity.

Croton Point, on the River's east bank, has been known to anglers *(above)* for centuries as an excellent fishing ground. The Hudson River natural historian Robert Boyle once heard from a local "striped bass fanatic" that "when the dogwoods are in bloom, it's time to cast [for bass]." Children dancing from rock to rock at Croton Point Park *(overleaf)* attest to the renewed cleanliness of the Hudson, auguring well for its future preservation.

The distinctive art forms of many diverse cultures have, over decades, been grafted onto the natural Hudson Valley landscape. At the Hammond Museum, in North Salem, an eclectic collection of art and memorabilia is set in the exquisite tranquility of a Japanese-style "stroll garden," where one can meditate, and be gently inspired. Radiant goldfish bring points of light to a stroll garden pond *(left)*, while a traditional lantern *(above)* marks a moment in one's walk.

"Shunpiking," that is, just meandering through the lower Hudson Valley's byways, can turn up the local color of a Nyack antique shop *(right)*, where a painted carousel horse may be for sale; or bring the traveler to the Renaissance Festival, held annually at Tuxedo *(above)*, where costumed revelers dance, play at jousting, and parley during summer weekends.

The Palisades Parkway leads
north from Nyack through
Rockland County to the
Hudson Highlands, one of
the few places on the North
American continent where a
river cuts through the
Appalachian mountain chain.
The highway, flung around
Bear Mountain *(above)* like a
ribbon, is but one avenue
from which to enjoy the
rustic beauty of the
Palisades; the Hudson River
Dayliner *(preceding page)* is
one of several floating
platforms in the River from
which the splendor of the
Highlands can be witnessed.

Chapter III
The Hudson Highlands

The Hudson as an essential artery connecting the interior with the ocean was recognized immediately by the Dutch. Later, in the eighteenth century, the River's potential as a strategic military barrier between New England and the Middle colonies was apprehensively noted—first during the French and Indian War when French Quebec was an adversary. This function of the River came to be crucial during the American Revolution when both the English and the Americans felt that whoever controlled the Hudson River Valley would control the colonies. Although the British did capture New York City and held it for the duration of the war, the Valley was kept free. A turning point, in fact, of the entire war was the Battle of Saratoga in October of 1777, when Horatio Gates and Benedict Arnold (still a loyal and determined American general) defeated the British general "Gentleman" Johnny Burgoyne.

After this, although precautions were taken to defend the River in various ways, including the establishment of Fort Putnam at West Point, and a mighty chain—forged of iron mined in the valley—which was strung across the River below West Point to keep British ships from sailing upstream, the British threat to the Valley was effectively ended. New York's first state senate met in a low stone house, preserved today, at Kingston; and General Washington, complaining that he was "without amusements or avocations... amongst these rugged and dreary mountains," spent the winter of 1782-1783 in the Hasbrouck house at Newburgh, waiting for official word that the peace treaty ending the war had been signed. Around Newburgh, the Hasbrouck house in its park-like setting, the Ellison mansion where General Henry Knox, General Horatio Gates and other Continental officers kept General Washington company, and the New Windsor Cantonment, where 8,000 soldiers camped during the winter of 1782-1783, are all restored today. At the New Windsor Cantonment a cluster of buildings offers exhibits and craft demonstrations which bring the existence of the hard-pressed Continental soldier to life, while occasionally on weekends men in blue and white Continental uniforms, like Rip Van Winkle seeming to be awakened perhaps from a sleep of two centuries, march through militia drills, fire muskets in celebration of American liberty, and then consume their rations by the light of lanterns.

West Point, which General Washington had called "the key to the continent" because of its strategic position on the River, was the site of Fort Putnam as well as one of the great phenomena of the Revolutionary War: the huge chain of iron links stretched across the Hudson on pontoons, which had been designed to keep the British ships from sailing upriver. The army corps of engineers continued to man the fort after the Revolution, and in 1802 the United States Military Academy was established at West Point.

The Military Academy by the time of the Civil War was the foremost engineering school in the Western Hemisphere. Today, with its alumni including Robert E. Lee, Ulysses S. Grant, George Armstrong Custer, "Black Jack" Pershing, Douglas MacArthur, George Patton, Dwight D. Eisenhower, and many other well-known and lesser-known former students (including James Abbott MacNeill Whistler, the painter) the Military Academy is a veritable monument to our national memories—of peace as well as war. It is also, of course, the training school of 4,500 male and female cadets.

West Point's lofty, austere buildings of gray West Point granite rise from the river cliffs (of which their stone was once part) like the battlements of a vast medieval castle. From the academy grounds, there is the famous view of the River coming down through the Highlands which gives one a very real sense of the River as a gateway to the interior of the continent. There is also the West Point Museum in Thayer Hall which contains dioramas of famous battles throughout history; exhibits demonstrating military life throughout American history; two hundred years of flags, posters, and uniforms; and local memorabilia, such as a model of the *Mary Powell*—the most famous steamboat on the river. Something to remember about West Point's Olympian atmosphere: until 1883 there were no railroads on the west bank of the Hudson, so, except for country roads, there was no approach to the plain except by river boat.

Across the River to the north, at Poughkeepsie, Vassar College, founded in 1861 by brewer—and later philanthropist—Matthew Vassar, was one of the first women's colleges in the world and, as such, was the sort of innovative American cultural institution which the Hudson Valley seemed to nurture. The central building of the college was designed by James Renwick, the famed nineteenth-century architect in the Gothic Revival style, who is also remembered for the Smithsonian Institution's "Castle" on the Mall in Washington and New York's St. Patrick's Cathedral.

Across from West Point on the eastern bank of the Hudson, near the charming river village of Cold Spring, sits the restored nineteenth-century mansion of Boscobel. Begun in 1805 by States Morris Dyckman, decandant of an old Dutch family, moved onto this site from Montrose and restored in the late 1950s by Lila Acheson Wallace, philanthropist and co-founder with her husband of *The Reader's Digest,* Boscobel represents a halcyon period of Hudson River civilization. When the mustard-colored walls and slender white Federal-style pillars of Boscobel were built, the hazards of the Revolution were over, and the bursting, brawling growth of the nineteenth century, marked by steamboats and high Gothic fantasies in architecture along the River's banks, had not yet happened. Nineteenth-century order and serenity lingered in the Duncan Phyfe furniture in Boscobel's parlors and in the formal parterres in the gardens.

Erratum
Page 49 should read

One contrast which makes the Boscobel formality so refreshing is the unspoiled wildness of the Highlands scenery on both sides of the River. In fact, from Bear Mountain in the south to Storm King in the north, the steep Highlands cliffs and their forests are protected, mostly, by state and private forest preserves. Bear Mountain State Park with its inn, built in 1915, lies at the southern entrance to the Highlands.

Bear Mountain State Park was created in 1910 when the Harriman family donated 10,000 acres to the state with the stipulation that the land would remain a wilderness area. The Harrimans also built the Bear Mountain Bridge. When it was completed in 1924, it was the first passenger car bridge across the Hudson south of Albany, and at that time it was the world's longest suspension bridge. Bear Mountain Bridge is now one of eight which cross the River south of Albany, from the George Washington Bridge (completed in 1931) to the Route 90 Bridge at Castleton-on-Hudson.

Deep in the Highlands area on the west bank of the River, there are two original American sites which represent the Hudson Valley's diversity: at Goshen the oldest harness track in America, now a national Historic Landmark, still trains trotters and pacers, as well as having a regular schedule of races at the nineteenth-century track with its wonderful, stick-style wooden grandstand. At Washingtonville the Brotherhood Winery, now one of twenty-five wineries in the Hudson Valley, carries on the tradition started by Huguenot settlers in the seventeenth-century. The Brotherhood Winery's underground wine cellars are the oldest—and still the largest—in the nation.

In marked contrast to these traditional activities, the Storm King Art Center in Mountainville is located in a French Norman-style mansion, built in the 1930s. Major twentieth-century sculptural work—including pieces by Isamu Noguchi, Alexander Calder, Henry Moore, and Louise Nevelson, among others—are located in the park-like grounds, as well as in the museum itself.

Another contrast to both the harness track and winery activities and the twentieth-century art at Storm King lies in the many craft fairs and antique shops which fill the small towns of both banks of the river all year round. In villages like nearly perfect Cold Spring, opposite West Point, there are many antique shops of varying quality, while in many towns on the west bank there are craft fairs throughout the summer at which the shunpiker can buy anything from a salad bowl carved from a single walnut branch to a handmade rag rug.

A seasonal delight which reflects the still vital importance of agriculture in the Valley are the county fairs which settle like agrarian brigadoons in the summer months. When the corn is ripe and the summer tomatoes are luscious and red, then the fairs open, large and vivid as sunflowers. County fairs throughout the Valley offer farmers and visitors a chance to see the biggest and best

spoiled wildness of the Highlands scenery on both sides of the River. In fact, from Bear Mountain in the south to Storm King in the north, the steep Highlands cliffs and their forests are protected, mostly, by state and private forest preserves. Bear Mountain State Park with its inn, built in 1915, lies at the southern entrance to the Highlands.

Bear Mountain State Park was created in 1910 when the Harriman family donated 10,000 acres to the state with the stipulation that the land would remain a wilderness area. The Harrimans also built the Bear Mountain Bridge. When it was completed in 1924, it was the first passenger car bridge across the Hudson south of Albany, and at that time it was the world's longest suspension bridge. Bear Mountain Bridge is now one of eight which cross the River south of Albany, from the George Washington Bridge (completed in 1931) to the Route 90 Bridge at Castleton-on-Hudson.

Deep in the Highlands area on the west bank of the River, there are two original American sites which represent the Hudson Valley's diversity: at Goshen the oldest harness track in America, now a national Historic Landmark, still trains trotters and pacers, as well as having a regular schedule of races at the nineteenth-century track with its wonderful, stick-style wooden grandstand. At Washingtonville the Brotherhood Winery, now one of twenty-five wineries in the Hudson Valley, carries on the tradition started by Huguenot settlers in the seventeenth-century. The Brotherhood Winery's underground wine cellars are the oldest—and still the largest—in the nation.

In marked contrast to these traditional activities, the Storm King Art Center in Mountainville is located in a French Norman-style mansion, built in the 1930s. Major twentieth-century sculptural work—including pieces by Isamu Noguchi, Alexander Calder, Henry Moore, and Louise Nevelson, among others—are located in the park-like grounds, as well as in the museum itself.

Another contrast to both the harness track and winery activities and the twentieth-century art at Storm King lies in the many craft fairs and antique shops which fill the small towns of both banks of the river all year round. In villages like nearly perfect Cold Spring, opposite West Point, there are many antique shops of varying quality, while in many towns on the west bank there are craft fairs throughout the summer at which the shunpiker can buy anything from a salad bowl carved from a single walnut branch to a handmade rag rug.

A seasonal delight which reflects the still vital importance of agriculture in the Valley are the county fairs which settle like agrarian brigadoons in the summer months. When the corn is ripe and the summer tomatoes are luscious and red, then the fairs open, large and vivid as sunflowers. County fairs throughout the Valley offer farmers and visitors a chance to see the biggest and best of the Valley's crops, take rides on the carnival attractions, witness a pig race, of the Valley's crops, take rides on the carnival attractions, witness a pig race, and—most importantly—realize the rich life which inhabits the Valley. Too often it is only the history of the Valley or its natural beauty which the visitor is directed to appreciate—both of them overwhelming, but neither fully indicative of the energy of the Valley's residents today.

Still, it is the beauty of the Hudson Highlands which lingers in the mind. From Bear Mountain to Storm King Mountain, the River narrows to a fraction of its widest point, the Tappan Zee—a mere fifteen miles or so to the south. Though the steep cliffs and rugged mountains which rise directly out of the River's banks would not be considered immense by the standards of, say, the Rocky Mountains—or even the Adirondacks—the dramatic scenery ranks among the most splendid in America.

The Highlands were formed thousands of years ago when the Hudson River cut through the Appalachian Mountain Range to form a craggy gorge. The River veers and curves through the Highlands, creating vistas of unparalleled majesty; mountain roads plunge and climb along the Hudson's banks, or wind tortuously along the face of steep mountain cliffs high above the water's surface. Violent storms develop suddenly in this region; often, in the cool early morning hours of summer days, or in the fall, when the scent of decaying leaves sweetens the air, the Highlands are bathed in a dense fog, rendering the already sublime beauty more breathtaking than could have been imagined.

The Hudson Highlands, seen in this way, may never be forgotten.

The Bear Mountain Bridge
(preceding page) forms the
gateway to the Hudson
Highlands. The longest
suspension bridge in the
world at the time of its
completion in 1924, the Bear
Mountain Bridge was the first
passenger car bridge across
the Hudson south of Albany.
The Bear Mountain Inn
(above) is a sylvan retreat
with civilized amenities
located in the state park land
donated to New York by the
Harriman family in 1910. An
antiques and crafts fair
(right) offers the park's
visitors an unusual setting in
which to find bargains.

State parks and protected areas such as Constitution Marsh *(above)*, opposite West Point, provide an environment in which recreation and ecological awareness have merged. The intricate ecosystem of the life-giving Hudson River marsh can be studied firsthand during canoe trips operated by the Audubon Society. Swimmers frolic in the pure lake water in Harriman State Park *(right)*.

From Castle Rock, high above the village of Garrison, the sweeping panorama of the Hudson Highlands *(opposite page)* takes in West Point and Storm King Mountain. Nestled in the bosom of the Hudson Highlands, guarded by mountains which the early Dutch settlers thought had mystical qualities, Garrison, in Putnam County, illustrates the peaceful beauty of life in the river villages. A nineteenth-century gazebo *(above)* is the centerpiece of the village's charming waterfront; few country clubs in the world offer such breathtaking vistas as this golf course near Garrison *(left)*.

The United States Military Academy at West Point was founded in 1802 to provide an elite corps of professionally trained military officers and engineers. The traditions of cadet life have been passed from class to class over nearly two centuries of discipline and study. Today, alumni review cadets *(opposite page)* who march in dress uniforms which recall West Point's early years; an enthusiastic war whoop announces that a plebe company *(above)* is present and accounted for during the rigorous "beast barracks" training. West Point's motto, "Duty, Honor, Country" finds symbolic expression on an Academy hall *(left)* built of local granite.

A modern "combat in the trenches," Army football games *(overleaf, top)* draw fans to Michie Stadium. The development of West Point as a stronghold during the American Revolution prevented the Hudson River Valley from suffering greatly from a different sort of combat; a restored Fort Putnam *(overleaf, bottom)* broods above West Point and the River it once guarded.

57

General George Washington, his key officers, and 8,000 men of the Continental Army spent the winter of 1782-83 at the New Windsor Cantonment, awaiting word that the peace treaty ending the war had been signed. The hardships of camp life *(left)* are not as extreme today, but the drills necessary to keep the militia ready for combat *(below)* are faithfully re-created.

Modern sculpture and ancient
forest dwarf visitors to the
Storm King Art Center
(above), in Mountainville.
Dozens of contemporary
works of art have been placed
around the wooded gardens
and in the Center's French-
Norman chateau. The
immortal landscapes of the
Hudson Highlands continue
to hold a fascination for
contemporary Valley
residents and visitors; hikers
rest on a scenic bluff
overlooking the River
(opposite page)
near West Point.

The estate surrounding Boscobel, the graceful Federal-style mansion near Garrison, calls to mind the order and serenity of the early-nineteenth century *(preceding pages)* amid the rugged splendor of the distant Taconic range, and the nearby Constitution Marsh. The beauty of Boscobel's exterior *(above)* was a refinement of eighteenth-century Georgian symmetry, before the severity of Greek Revival and the fantastic shapes of Victorian Gothic took over building styles. A bedstead attributed to Duncan Phyfe, the Federal cabinetmaker, rests in Elizabeth Dyckman's chamber *(left)*; in the tulip bed beside the orangerie *(opposite page)*, beehives provide a note of industry among the flowers.

The quiet streets of Hudson River Valley villages such as Cold Spring *(above)* are charming places to search for antiques and to escape from the pressures of modern city life; after hunting for bargains at one of the many quaint shops *(left)* to be found in Cold Spring, country inns like the Hudson House *(opposite page)* provide a comfortable place to spend the night.

The Newburgh-Beacon
Bridge *(right)* is one of the
busiest crossings over the
Hudson. The ease with which
the River can be crossed has
made attractions such as the
Goshen Historic Track in
Orange County *(above)*,
accessible from all parts of
the Valley. Now a National
Historic Landmark, the track
at Goshen is the oldest
harness track in America.

Traditional art forms and
contemporary disciplines
often blend in unusual ways
in the Valley; a martial arts
group *(above)* performs with
geometric precision on the
pier at Newburgh Landing,
while at Beacon *(left)*, Morris
dancers invoke ritual
movements and rhythms
during Clearwater's
Strawberry Festival.

The Taconic State Parkway
(preceding pages) stretches
from Westchester County to
northern Columbia County;
the richness of fall's colors
along its path rivals New
England for sheer splendor.

A Sunday boat race *(above)*
at the Chelsea Yacht Club,
near Beacon, demonstrates
the sporting life which has
attracted people to the River
for centuries. The IBM plant
at Poughkeepsie *(opposite
page)* is an example of
contemporary industry which
has made the Hudson Valley
prosperous while also
assuming responsibility for
the ecological and cultural
balance of the region.

Vassar College, founded in
Poughkeepsie in 1861 by
philanthropist Matthew
Vassar, is one of the Valley's
great cultural institutions.
The college's first building
was designed by James
Renwick, architect of the
Smithsonian's "Castle" and
St. Patrick's Cathedral;
today, the campus blends
modern architecture with
the classic structure
(above).

Autumn is the season to "pick-your-own" in the Hudson River Valley; apples *(top, left)* and pumpkins *(bottom, left)* are perennial favorites in the fields near Marlboro. Agriculture in the Valley has always been cultivated on a small but profitable basis; fruit stands *(above, left)* abound in the region, while another thriving Valley industry is wine-making. New York State labels *(above, right)* such as these, in the wine cellar at the Brotherhood Winery in Washingtonville, enjoy an enthusiastic clientele throughout the nation.

North of the Hudson
Highlands, the land becomes
flatter *(opposite page)*, more
suited to agriculture—the
basis of wealth for the old
Hudson River Valley
families. The autumn harvest
(above) composes a timeless
landscape; such scenes have
been the inspiration for
Hudson Valley artists
for centuries.

Chapter IV
The Great Estates Region

The upper Hudson Valley, with its luminous atmosphere beloved by the artists of the Hudson River School, its rolling hills and scenic mountains—still undeveloped for the most part—and its great estates, many of which have been maintained either publicly or privately as they originally were, has the quality of a land which has been civilized for centuries. It is, in a word, pastoral. This was the country of the great, mostly later nineteenth-century estates, where Gothic mansions, outsize Victorian castles and marble palaces were built by old Dutch families and *nouveaux riches* railroad tycoons alike.

Hyde Park is a Hudson River town where Franklin Delano Roosevelt's family estate is located. The mansion's name is actually "Springwood," and, although the estate is known usually as "Hyde Park," there are several other important mansions near the town. The mansion "Hyde Park" is, of course, far and away the most important historically, and it is where the greatest sense of life has survived, despite a bad fire at the mansion itself in January 1982. The complex at Roosevelt's Hyde Park consists of the mansion which FDR's father bought in 1867 and which was extensively remodeled in Federal style by FDR and his mother Sara Delano Roosevelt in 1915; the stone library with FDR's presidential papers and his private collection on the history of Dutchess County and the Hudson River Valley; and the cottage known as Val-Kill, which was Eleanor's personal retreat from the 1930s on and her home for the last seventeen years of her life.

Mrs. Roosevelt said in a small memoir about Hyde Park that "the front porch has memories of a very particular kind, for this is where my husband always stood with his mother to greet important guests. It is where she always met him when he arrived for a visit, and on this porch he stood when his friends and neighbors came to congratulate him after each nomination and on every election night."

Hyde Park, of course, was visited when the Roosevelts lived there by King George VI and Queen Elizabeth of England, Nikita Khrushchev, Jawaharlal Nehru, and John F. Kennedy, among other world leaders. Franklin and Eleanor Roosevelt are buried in the rose garden.

Franklin Roosevelt's family were old Dutch settlers in the Valley, and they owned land around Poughkeepsie and Hyde Park for four generations before Franklin's birth. The President could remember his grandfather singing him a nursery rhyme in Dutch which the grandfather had heard from *his* great-grandfather. Roosevelt suggested to Carl Carmer, who interviewed him in the 1930s for Carmer's book *The Hudson,* that the author should include a chapter called "Vaulting Ambition." Referring to some typical Hudson River gentry, he said, "Here is a family who must have a replica of the Petit Trianon built in marble on the banks of the Hudson at the cost of millions . . . ." Two of the mansions which could be said to represent "Vaulting Ambition" are near the town of Hyde Park. They are fascinating pieces of architectural history although they don't have a patch on the Roosevelt mansion for real, lived history, both domestic and grand.

The Mills Mansion, which belonged to Ogden Mills—whose family had made a fortune in banking in California—was completed in 1896 and was designed by the great architectural firm of McKim, Mead & White, well known for New York City's old Pennsylvania Station. Ogden Mills also owned houses in Paris, Newport, New York City, and California, so this house had little life in it to humanize its grandeur. It retains, however, Flemish tapestries, gilded plasterwork, marble, and oak paneling, which are fine examples of turn-of-the-century "Vaulting Ambition."

The Vanderbilts tore down an elegant Federal house at Hyde Park in the 1890s to build a marble mansion, also designed by McKim, Mead & White. Frederick Vanderbilt, who built the house, kept 3 million dollars in his checking account ("in case I want to buy something," he said), and the house and decoration, when it was completed in 1899, cost just about that much. The Vanderbilt Mansion is an extremely formal house. The interiors were partly decorated by Ogden Codman, who wrote a turn-of-the-century book called *The Decoration of Houses*. This book was noteworthy for two things: firstly, Codman's co-author was Edith Wharton and "Decoration" was her first published work; and, secondly, the book was the first more-or-less modern book on interiors to point out that decoration and architecture must go hand in hand.

Farther north on the east bank there are two mansions which, although very different from each other, both represent ties to the Hudson which are more integral than those of the grand marble palaces. Clermont, near Germantown, was part of the Livingston family estate from 1686 until 1962. The Livingstons were one of the great old Hudson River Valley families from the time patriarch Robert married Alida Schuyler Van Rensselaer in 1679, and the house at Clermont replaced one which was burned in the Revolution. This mansion had a new French-Renaissance style peaked roof added in the 1870s and remains today the gracious center of a 450-acre estate, close to the banks of the River. Clermont's name was taken for the first successful steamboat in history, which was developed partly by Robert R. Livingston in partnership with Robert Fulton and which first chugged up the Hudson, as all the world knows, in 1807.

Olana, just south of Hudson, was built by the great luminist painter Frederic Edward Church in 1874. It is a grand Moorish-Victorian fantasy set high on a hill. Church himself said of the house, "It is like what the old woman said of her mock turtle soup, 'I made it out of me own head.'" The house, full of Victorian gimcracks, was constructed of glazed tiles, polychromed brick, and colored slate. It is completely an artist's private vision, but the vision of an artist who was intimately related to the Hudson Valley. The views from the house of the River and the Catskill Mountains make an ever-changing live Hudson River landscape, the original of Church's famous paintings.

One of the most beautiful of the great estates, Montgomery Place, in the hamlet of Annandale-on-Hudson, is presently under restoration. The estate which Andrew Jackson Downing, the prominent nineteenth-century landscape architect, said was "nowhere surpassed in America in location, natural beauty, or landscape gardening charms," remained in the hands of Livingston family descendants from 1805 until 1986. Sleepy Hollow Restorations has acquired the property and plans to open the estate to the public in 1988. Until then, travelers to the northern Dutchess County area must content themselves with visiting the Montgomery Place orchards and fruit stand.

In addition to its stately mansions, historic estates, and cultural shrines, the Great Estates region of the Valley contains some delightful curiosities. The beautiful town of Rhinebeck is home to an esoteric amusement which is also a unique living museum. The old Rhinebeck Aerodrome has a collection of airplanes from World War I and earlier which are actually used on Saturdays and Sundays from May through October to stage mock air battles. It is possible to take a private ride in an open-cockpit plane out over the Hudson and experience the thrills and excitement of early flight yourself, as well as getting a view of the River and the mountains which even Frederic Church never had.

In the town of Hudson, New York, The American Museum of Firefighting, another delight of the Valley, contains firefighting equipment which dates back to 1725 and includes resplendent nineteenth-century fire engines, some of which were so elegant they were never used at a fire, but only in parades.

On the west side of the Hudson, some miles back from the River, lies New Paltz, founded by the Huguenots (French Protestant refugees who came to the Valley from Germany, to which they had previously fled) in 1678. Huguenot Street in New Paltz has six restored stone houses from the late-seventeenth century. At Kingston, about fifteen miles to the north and on the River, the Senate House, another low-built ancient stone homestead, was the seat of the first Senate of New York State in the fall of 1777. In October of 1777 the British burned Kingston, but this building, although damaged, was not completely destroyed. Today it has an adjacent museum which contains Hudson River memorabilia, as well as a collection of paintings by John Vanderlyn, an early nineteenth-century landscape painter and portraitist and a protege of Aaron Burr's.

The west bank of the Hudson is dominated, geographically and to some extent culturally, by the Catskill Mountains. Known today as the home of resorts popular with many New York City people, historically the Catskills were considered a thinly populated wilderness with one or two classic old resort hotels.

The sparse population of the Catskill area has been traditionally regarded with the suspicion and romance usually associated with folk from the Appalachian hills and hollows. Descendants of renegades who fled the safe but confining patroonships along the River, or descendants of Loyalists who fraternized with the British during the Revolution, the Catskill Valley settlers were known by such names as "Pondshiners" and "Eagle Nesters," and, as late as the 1930s, according to Carl Carmer, they allegedly practiced witchcraft.

Rising far above the hollows were two grand old resort hotels, one of which still lives. The Catskill Mountain House—closed in 1942 and burned in 1963—was the grander of the two. It had a view from the piazza that stretched up and down the Hudson which wound like a silver ribbon through the valley 2,200 feet below. Everyone spoke of the view as sublime (in the classic sense of the word, meaning "morally elevating"), and Harriet Martineau, an English lady traveler who normally looked on American institutions as less than elevating, said she would rather have missed Niagara.

However, the traveler still can appreciate the Mohonk Mountain House today, which lies on the west slope of a mountain behind New Paltz. Run since 1870 by the Quaker Smiley family, this vast Victorian pile runs along the mountain side between the slope and a black water mountain tarn. The views are spectacular and the Victorian atmosphere virtually undiluted.

Sitting on the Mohonk veranda in the gloaming, rocking and watching the sun turn the rounded distant mountain tops purple, is far from the worst way to appreciate this lovely part of the Hudson Valley. Here, it is possible to believe that the ghost of Rip Van Winkle still dwells in the rarefied atmosphere of the mysterious Catskill Mountains.

The familiar profile *(inset)* of a great president awaits visitors to Franklin Delano Roosevelt's ancestral home at Hyde Park. The mansion *(above)* had been bought by FDR's father and remodeled by Roosevelt and his mother in a grand Federal style in 1915. Flowers layed by family members dignify the grave of Eleanor Roosevelt, located near Franklin's in the rose garden *(left)* at Hyde Park. His office and library *(opposite page)* contain both presidential papers and a private collection of Hudson Valley lore.

The grandeur of the
Vanderbilt Mansion's
architecture *(above)*
counterpoints the natural
beauty of the nearby Hudson
River and the distant outline
of the Catskill Mountains.
Unlike the long-established
River families, whose wealth
and power were derived from
the land on which they lived,
the Vanderbilt's fortune came
from beyond the Valley; the
opulent Vanderbilt dining
room *(opposite page)* reflects
a taste in the decorative
arts which is not native
to the region.

No longer exclusive retreats for the wealthy and powerful, Vanderbilt Mansion *(below)* and Clermont *(right)* provide lovely settings in which to picnic amid fall's splendor or to enjoy a summertime concert.

87

The Mills Mansion *(preceding page, top)*, in Staatsburg, commands a magnificent view of the Hudson River. Portraits of Livingston family members *(preceding page, bottom left)* hang in poignant contrast to the elaborate furnishings within the mansion *(preceding page, bottom right)*.

A solitary bee hovers above the elegant landscape of Montgomery Place *(opposite page)*; while the mansion undergoes restoration, the orchards *(above)* provide a variety of apples, pears and other fruits for picking on the estate.

Olana, the home of nineteenth-century landscape artist Frederic Church, was situated to take advantage of a Hudson Valley landscape *(left)* as grand as any of Church's own paintings. The Moorish-style fantasy *(opposite page, bottom)* reflects Victorian tastes; the seemingly chaotic nature of Olana's interiors *(below)* are more a reflection of the artist's unique private vision.

91

French Huguenots founded New Paltz, on the Hudson's west bank, in 1678; the surviving stone houses lie along one of the oldest streets in America *(above)*. The finely detailed window and gable *(right)* on a house in Rhinebeck give substance to the term "Hudson River Gothic," coined by novelist Edith Wharton to describe nineteenth-century Valley architecture.

Summer is the season of festivals and fairs in the Valley; at the Dutchess County Fair, in Rhinebeck, the thrill of carnival rides *(opposite page)* is matched only by the eager anticipation of young farmers *(inset)* waiting for their livestock to be judged.

Although the Hudson remains a vital commercial thoroughfare, it is also a river made for recreation. Near the Esopus Lighthouse *(left)*, a tanker steams toward port; water skiing *(above)* is a favorite summer sport.

95

Adding a note of whimsy to the upper Hudson River Valley, the Old Rhinebeck Aerodrome *(opposite page, bottom)* and the American Museum of Firefighting *(below)*, in Hudson, are delightful contrasts to the historic houses and cultural shrines usually associated with the region. From the cockpit of one of the Aerodrome's biplanes *(opposite page, top)*, the beautiful town of Rhinebeck will fade into a Hudson Valley landscape not even Frederic Church could have imagined.

The Mohonk
Mountain House
(left), near New
Paltz, was built in
1870 by the Smiley
family, who still
own it today.
Perched 1,200 feet
above the Hudson
Valley on the edge
of a mountain tarn,
this hotel is one of
the great surviving
Victorian resorts.
Golf, tennis,
swimming, riding,
concerts and
mind-improving
lectures are all
offered in the
refreshing
atmosphere of the
Catskills, and in
one of the best
preserved and
functioning
Victorian interiors
in the nation.
Beside the resort's
pond, a guest
(above) may find
the time to read or
think in the bracing
mountain air.

The modern technology that
permitted great bridges, such
as the Kingston-Rhinecliff
crossing *(above)*, to span
the River sometimes had an
adverse effect when industrial
wastes polluted sections of
the Hudson; today, beaches
and natural wildlife preserves
along the River from New
York City to Albany are
beginning to flourish again.
Children swim in the Hudson
at an Ulster County beach
(right); the Livingston Marsh
(opposite page) traces a
serpentine path to
the Hudson.

The Hudson Valley can be a
wonderful place for children,
in all seasons. At the Catskill
Game Farm *(opposite page,
top)* in Catskill, a child pets
a deer which roams freely
through the compound; at
Hunter Mountain, a ski
lesson *(opposite page,
bottom)* takes place in the
clean winter snow. At a small
circus in the town of Leeds,
there is a more traditional
entertainment for children;
acrobats perform death-
defying feats *(above)*
and circus animals court
young audiences under
the "Big Top."

Held beneath one of the largest tents in the world *(below)*, the German Alps Festival is just one of the many ethnic festivals celebrated at Hunter Mountain each summer.

The magnificent backdrop of the Catskill Mountains dominates the west side of the River. Skiers *(overleaf, left)* make their downhill runs at Hunter Mountain, in Greene County; in another season, near Kingston in Ulster County, sunset illuminates the pleasures of an evening's sail *(overleaf, right)* on the Hudson River.

Chapter V
The Capital District and Saratoga

Henry James at the turn-of-the-century compared Albany to some "placid rich-voiced gentlewoman," while Alice Roosevelt Longworth, reminiscing about the same era when her father Theodore was governor of New York State, said that living in Albany was like living in an Anthony Trollope novel, all Episcopalian clergymen and tea. Neither of these well-bred people would recognize the Albany of William Kennedy, whose fictional *Albany Trilogy,* published in the last decade, portrayed a city of earthy human survivor types. And neither of these pictures—old genteel Albany, nor Kennedy's decaying Albany of the years after World War II—anticipated the busy port city of today with its grand Empire State Plaza looming over the river front.

Albany, founded by the Dutch as Fort Orange in 1624, stands at the head of the navigable channel of the Hudson, 150 miles from the sea. It has been a strategic location, bridging transatlantic trade and the interior of the continent, since the Dutch traded there for furs with the Indians. In 1797 Albany became the state capital. At that time it was a small city, Old World in feeling, with housewives scrubbing their stoops every day and church sermons still preached in Dutch. In 1825 the Erie Canal opened. The canal ran from Albany to Buffalo and it transformed Albany, the River, and even New York City.

Today, Albany is the nation's sixth largest port, thanks to the River. It is also the home of the world's largest publicly owned collection of contemporary art in the Empire State Plaza, as well as being the location of the New York State Museum and the Albany Institute of History and Art.

The State Capitol building is an architectural feast. Built over a period of more than thirty years (1867-1898) at a cost of more than 25 million in nineteenth-century dollars, the building was designed by three architects. Thomas Fuller, known for the Gothic revival parliament buildings in Ottawa, Canada, began the design and was succeeded by Leopold Eidlitz and H.H. Richardson, working independently. Eidlitz—like Fuller—worked in the Gothic mode, with a predilection for Near Eastern ornament, while Richardson perfected the heavy and dignified forms of Romanesque revival. Although Richardson and Eidlitz collaborated on the exterior, each worked on separate parts of the interior, making the building an extremely rich collection of late Victorian styles and materials. On the Great Western Staircase, known as "the million dollar staircase," the heads of figures from New York State history and legends are carved.

The State Capitol today is integrated into the very modern Governor Nelson A. Rockefeller Empire State Plaza. This complex of office buildings, a 44-story tower, legislative and judicial office buildings, and the Performing Arts Center (known as "The Egg"), was begun in 1962 and completed in 1978. The chief architect was Wallace K. Harrison, who had been chairman of the board of architects for both the United Nations Headquarters and Lincoln Center in New York City. The complex sits on a platform a quarter-of-a-mile long which is itself a five-story building. From the river front, its facade rises like the Palisades or the cliffs of the Highlands downriver; within are shops and the art collection which Nelson Rockefeller initiated while he was governor. The permanent art collection which lines the Concourse includes paintings and sculptures created by such leading artists as Isamu Noguchi, Robert Motherwell, and Louise Nevelson. The New York State Museum, located at the southern end of the Plaza, offers permanent and changing exhibitions about New York State life and history.

A contrast to the Empire State Plaza in almost every way, the Albany Institute of History and Art, housed in a red brick turn-of-the-century building, is one of the most elegant small museums in the nation. With an unparalleled collection of eighteenth-century portraits, Hudson River School art, furniture and other artifacts from the Hudson Valley, the Albany Institute offers an aesthetic respite from the bustling pace of the capital.

Hudson River historian Allan Keller called General Philip Schuyler's mansion, "The Pastures," "one of the finest examples of American Georgian architecture to be found in the world." Built in 1762, The Pastures was constructed of mellow red brick and designed with the exquisite Georgian symmetry and balance so natural to the Age of Enlightenment. Details such as the Chinoiserie railing on the balustrade around the roof are rarely found in American houses. Furniture from the Colonial and Federal periods fills the house, including the formal drawing room in which Alexander Hamilton married the General's daughter Elizabeth in 1780.

On the east bank of the Hudson, below Albany and north of the town of Hudson, lies the quaint village of Kinderhook, near which stands Lindenwald, the Federal-style mansion bought by Martin Van Buren in 1839, while he was President. Van Buren's son hired architect Richard Upjohn, one of the first practitioners of the Gothic revival in America, in 1848 to "Italianate" the mansion, so that today it boasts a tuscan tower and cornice, making it an example of Hudson River Gothic grafted onto an earlier style.

To the east of Kinderhook the Shaker Museum at Old Chatham preserves the furniture, tools, crafts, and rooms of this millenialist sect. As with the innovative programs at West Point and Vassar, and the extra-orthodox beliefs of the Huguenots at New Paltz, so for the Shakers the Hudson Valley was a tolerant and nurturing home. The Shakers' beliefs in celibacy and the equality of men and women were looked at askance by their neighbors, but their good produce, elegantly simple furniture and hospitality were favorably regarded without qualification. Between 1776 and the present—two tiny communities in New England survive—there have been approximately 17,000 Shakers, and they exemplify one of the best—if one of the more extreme—examples of life, liberty and the pursuit of happiness in the New World.

North of Albany, the Hudson River meanders through pastoral plains to Saratoga National Park, the location of the Battle of Saratoga in October 1777. It was here that General Horatio Gates of the Continental Army defeated General Burgoyne, known as "Gentleman Johnny," Commander of His Majesty's Troops, thus halting the British plan of dividing the colonies into two parts along the line of the Hudson River.

Ten miles north of the battlefield, Saratoga Springs waits for the annual influx of summer visitors which it has welcomed since 1800. The first big hotel in Saratoga was erected about that time by Gideon Putnam, who advertised that the springs had rejuvenating power, good for body and spirit. For the next 130 years, Saratoga was the most famous resort in the United States, giving its name to a trunk and to the first potato chip (known originally as the "Saratoga chip"). During the Civil War a racetrack was opened at Saratoga, and it became not only fashionable, but "racy." Over the century-and-a-half of its popularity, Saratoga has been host to everyone from Martin Van Buren, when he was President, to Diamond Jim Brady and Lillian Russell. Today, although the town has lost several of its glorious old Victorian hotels, it is home to the Saratoga Performing Arts Center and during the month of August, High Society still finds it a great day for the races there.

From the river front, site of one of the nation's busiest ports *(left)*, the Empire State Plaza *(above)* rises above Albany like the Palisades or the cliffs of the Hudson Highlands downriver.

In rural Columbia County, not far from the state capital, the pastoral beauty of the Valley has not been altered by encroaching development. The town of Chatham *(above)* offers a still-life awash in autumn hues; in a spontaneous celebration of life, a horse *(left)* rolls exuberantly in the early morning dew.

The sedate, peaceful air of the Hudson River Valley seems to inspire the creative impulses of its residents, and to nurture social experiments. Lindenwald, Martin Van Buren's home *(opposite page)* near Kinderhook, possesses a sense of quiet strength due, in large part, to the dignified blend of Gothic and Italianate style in its architecture. Exquisite craftsmanship and simple beauty *(below)* were the hallmarks of Shaker life; the Shaker Museum in Old Chatham *(left)* preserves the furniture and tools of the millennialist sect.

The Governor Nelson A. Rockefeller Empire State Plaza *(preceding pages)*, in Albany, is not only the site of state government but the scene for many festivals and celebrations throughout the year. The modern Performing Arts Center ("The Egg") and the Gothic State Capitol building express the evolution of architectural styles in the Valley.

A Fourth of July ethnic festival held in the Plaza finds exhilarant participants enacting traditional folktales *(above)*; logging in the Adirondacks *(opposite page, bottom)* is the subject of one of several permanent and changing exhibitions offered by the New York State Museum; the permanent sculpture collection which lines the Plaza *(opposite page, top)*, and the paintings in the Concourse, include works by leading international artists.

A marked contrast to the
ultra-modern Empire State
Plaza, General Philip
Schuyler's home, "The
Pastures," was constructed
of mellow red brick and
designed with the exquisite
symmetry typical of
Georgian architecture
(above).

Visitors to exclusive Saratoga Springs enjoy a luxurious brunch *(left)* at the Gideon Putnam Hotel, or savor a sumptuous champagne supper in front of the Performing Arts Center *(below)*. During the month of August each year, the resort town becomes the thoroughbred racing capital of America *(overleaf)*.

Chapter VI
The North Country

North of Saratoga the old lumbering and paper mill towns of Cohoes and Glens Falls signal the beginning of rough water on the River and the beginning of the mountains. In the Adirondacks, the actual course of the Hudson is quite often inaccessible, except to hikers. Much of the Adirondack wilderness—nearly six million acres, an area greater than the entire State of New Jersey—has been permanently protected since the 1890s as part of the Adirondack Park. The life of the great summer "camps" of the rich with their self-consciously rustic lodges filled with Adirondack furniture has been preserved in the Adirondack Museum at Blue Mountain Lake.

It was these camps which sheltered the nation's richest families in rustic luxury. As early as the 1880s five acres of land on one of the fashionable Adirondack lakes sold for $20,000. (And this was when a laborer's income could be as little as a dollar a day and in the West land was free for the settling on it under the Homestead Act.) Despite the excesses of thirty room log cabins filled with pool tables and oriental rugs, it was due in no small part to the deep affection these wealthy "homesteaders" felt for the Adirondacks that they became the protected wilderness they remain today.

Although much of the region has been designated "forever wild" by the State, the Adirondacks remain one of the most popular destinations for wilderness fans in America. The clear mountain waters and the rough peaks of the Adirondacks draw campers, hikers, mountain climbers, and water sports enthusiasts to the region; many come today just to enjoy the majestic panoramas or to revel in the fresh clean air of the north country.

A surveyor named Verplanck Colvin who began work in the 1870s charted the Adirondacks for much of his life. In one of his reports to the New York State Legislature, he wrote: "Elsewhere are mountains more stupendous, more icy and more drear, but none look down upon a grander landscape...more brightly gemmed with innumerable lakes or crystal pools...." In 1872 Colvin realized that one of those little pools on the side of Mount Marcy was the ultimate source of the Hudson River. He wrote that it was "a minute, unpretending tear of the clouds" and named it accordingly Lake Tear of the Clouds. From this droplet came the mighty Hudson, and in Colvin's phrase there is the implication that, like all great myths, the Hudson has a true origin in the heavens.

In the Adirondacks, the
actual course of the Hudson
River is quite often
inaccessible, except to hikers
and intrepid white-water
enthusiasts, who ride the
rough water on inner tubes.
Ardent golfers have planted a
course by the Hudson's
banks, against the backdrop
of the Adirondack Preserve's
6,000,000 acres *(preceding pages)*.
Lake Tear of the Clouds
(above) is the source of
the Hudson River; in its
name there is the implication
that the River has its true
origin in the heavens.

For the Visitors' Reference

Directory of Tourism Agencies

A variety of travel guides and directories are available to travelers planning a trip to the Hudson River Valley. Call or write for information regarding special events, accommodations, restaurants, and complete listings of the many historic sites and attractions which make the Valley such a unique place to visit or live in.

Adirondack North Country Association
Adirondack, New York 12808
(518) 494-2515

Albany County Convention & Visitors Bureau
600 Broadway
Albany, New York 12207
(518) 434-1217

Arts Council of Rockland, Inc. (ACOR)
Rockland County Health Center
Pomona, New York 10970
(914) 354-8400

Bed & Breakfast USA
Box 606
Croton-on-Hudson, New York 10520
(914) 271-6228

Columbia County Chamber of Commerce
729 Columbia Street
Hudson, New York 12534
(518) 828-4417

Dutchess County Arts Council
39 Market Street
Poughkeepsie, New York 12601
(914) 454-3222

Dutchess County Tourism Promotion Agency
46 Albany Post Road
P.O. Box 2025
Hyde Park, New York 12538
(914) 229-0033

Eastern Orange Chamber of Commerce
47 Grand Street
Newburgh, New York 12550
(914) 562-5100

Greene County Promotion Department
P.O. Box 467
Catskill, New York 12414
(518) 943-3223

Hudson River Regional Wine Council
R.D. 2, Box 36
Pine Bush, New York 12566
(914) 744-2226

Hudson River Valley Association
72 Main Street
Cold Spring-on-Hudson, New York 10516
(914) 265-3066

Hudson Valley Information Center
Franklin D. Roosevelt National Historic Site Home & Library
Route 9
Hyde Park, New York 12538

Mid-Hudson Chapter, New York State Restaurant Association
c/o Dick Smith's Restaurant
313 Manchester Road
Poughkeepsie, New York 12603
(914) 473-3045

New York Convention & Visitors Bureau, Inc.
Two Columbus Circle
New York, New York 10019
(212) 397-8200

New York State Department of Commerce
Division of Tourism
1 Commerce Plaza
Albany, New York 12245
(800) CALL-NYS

New York State Department of Commerce
Division of Tourism
One Albany Avenue
Kingston, New York 12401
(914) 331-6415

New York State Hotel and Motel Association
40 W. 38th Street
New York, New York 10018
(212) 921-8888

Office of General Services, Empire State Plaza Visitor Assistance
Concourse Room 106
Empire State Plaza
Albany, New York 12242
(518) 474-2418

Orange County Tourist Promotion Agency
124 Main Street
Goshen, New York 10924
(914) 294-5151

Putnam County Tourism
72 Main Street
Cold Spring-on-Hudson, New York 10516
(914) 265-3066

Rockland County Tourism
145 College Road
Suffern, New York 10901
(914) 356-4650, ext. 479

Saratoga County Promotion Director
40 McMaster Street
Ballston Spa, New York 12020
(518) 885-5381

The Sullivan County Catskills
Office of Public Information and Publicity
County Government Center
Monticello, New York 12701
(914) 794-3000

Sullivan County Community College, Travel and
  Tourism Department
Loch Sheldrake, New York 12759
(914) 434-5750

Thruway Information Centers
P.O. Box 91
Malden-on-Hudson, New York 12453
(914) 246-8453

Ulster County Public Information
P.O. Box 1800
Kingston, New York 12401
(914) 331-9300

Westchester Tourism Council
148 Martine Avenue
White Plains, New York 10601
(914) 285-2941

State and National Parks and Sites in the Hudson River Valley

The Hudson River Valley is home to beautiful parks and camp-grounds, hiking trails, nature centers, picnic grounds and recreation areas, and historic sites and battlefields. For information regarding seasons, fees, and facilities, call or write any of the tourism agencies serving the Hudson River Valley, or the following:

New York State Office of Parks, Recreation
  and Historic Preservation
Albany, New York 12238
(518) 474-0456

Office of Parks, Recreation and Historic Preservation
Taconic Region
Staatsburg, New York 12580
(914) 889-4100

Palisades Interstate Park Commission
Bear Mountain State Park
Bear Mountain, New York 10911
(914) 786-2701

Saratoga-Capital State Park, Recreation and
  Historic Preservation Region
Box W
Saratoga Springs, New York 12866
(518) 584-2000

Visitors Information Center
United States Military Academy
West Point, New York 10996
(914) 938-2638

The name and location of state and national parks and sites which can be found in the Hudson River Valley are listed below. For complete information, address inquiries to the preceding information centers and tourism agencies.

Adirondack Park

James Baird State Park
Pleasant Valley

Bear Mountain State Park
Bear Mountain

Catskill Park

Cherry Plain Area
Stephentown

Clermont State Historic Park
Germantown

Clarence Fahnestock Memorial State Park
Cold Spring

Franklin and Eleanor Roosevelt National Historic Site
Hyde Park

Franklin D. Roosevelt State Park
Yorktown Heights

Goshen Historic Track
Goshen

Grafton Lakes State Park
Troy

Harriman State Park
  Beaver Pond
  Lake Kanawauke
  Lake Sebago
  Lake Tiorati
  Lake Welch
  Sebago Rental Cabins
  Silver Mine
  Anthony Wayne Area
Harriman

High Tor State Park
Haverstraw

Hudson Highlands State Park
Beacon

Huguenot Houses
New Paltz

John Jay Homestead State Historic Site
Katonah

Knox Headquarters State Historic Site
Newburgh

Lake Taghkanic State Park
Ancram

Madam Brett Homestead
Beacon

Mills Mansion State Historic Site
Staatsburg

Mills Memorial State Park
Staatsburg

Moreau Lake State Park
South Glens Falls

New Windsor Cantonment State Historic Site
Newburgh (Vail's Gate)

Margaret Lewis Norrie State Park
Staatsburg

Nyack Beach State Park
Nyack

Olana State Historic Site
Hudson

Philipse Manor Hall State Historic Site
Yonkers

Rockefeller State Park Preserve
Pocantico Hills

Rockland Lake State Park
Congers

Saratoga National Historical Park
Stillwater

Saratoga Spa State Park
Saratoga Springs

Schuyler Mansion State Historic Site
Albany

Senate House State Historic Site
Kingston

Stony Point Battlefield State Historic Site
Stony Point

Taconic State Park, Copake Falls Area
Copake Falls

Taconic State Park, Rudd Pond Area
Millerton

Tallman Mountain State Park
Piermont

John Boyd Thacher State Park
Albany

Thompson's Lake Camping Area
Albany

Martin Van Buren National Historic Site
Kinderhook

Vanderbilt Mansion National Historic Site
Hyde Park

Van Wyck Homestead Museum
Fishkill

Washington's Headquarters
   (Jonathan Hasbrouck House State Historic Site)
Newburgh

A Hudson River Valley Library

The books cited below are representative of the literature which has been published over the years about the Hudson River Valley. By no means an exhaustive list, this library is intended to provide interested readers with additional sources of information about the history, architecture, and art of the Hudson River Valley.

Adams, Arthur G. *The Hudson: A Guidebook to the River.* Albany: State University of New York Press, 1981.

——————————. *The Hudson River in Literature: An Anthology.* Albany: State University of New York Press, 1980.

Andrews, Wayne. *American Gothic.* New York: Random House, 1975.

Boyle, Robert. *The Hudson River: A Natural and Unnatural History.* New York: W.W. Norton, 1969.

Butler, Joseph T. *Sleepy Hollow Restorations: A Cross-Section of the Collection.* Tarrytown, N.Y.: Sleepy Hollow Press, 1982.

Carmer, Carl. *The Hudson River.* New York: Farrar & Rinehart, 1939.

Davis, Alexander Jackson. *Rural Residences.* New York: New York University, 1837. Reprinted with new introduction by Jane B. Davies, New York: Da Capo Press, 1980.

Downing, Andrew Jackson. *Architecture of Country Houses.* New York: Appleton, 1850.

Folsom, Merrill. *Great American Mansions.* New York: Hastings House, 1963.

Howat, John K. *Hudson River and its Painters.* New York: The Viking Press, 1962.

Irving, Washington. *Rip Van Winkle & The Legend of Sleepy Hollow.* Tarrytown, N.Y.: Sleepy Hollow Press, 1980.

James, Henry. *The American Scene.* Bloomington: Indiana University Press, 1905.

Keller, Allan. *Life Along the Hudson.* Tarrytown, N.Y.: Sleepy Hollow Press, 1985.

Kennedy, William. *Ironweed.* New York: The Viking Press, 1983.

Landmarks of Dutchess County, 1683–1867: Architecture Worth Saving in New York State. New York: New York State Council on the Arts, 1969.

Lossing, Benson J. *The Hudson: From the Wilderness to the Sea.* Troy: Nims and Co., 1866.

Milbert, Jacques. *Picturesque Itinerary of the Hudson River.* Originally published in Paris in 1828–29. Reprinted, Ridgewood, N.J.: Gregg Press, 1968.

Mulligan, Tim. *The Hudson River Valley: A History and Guide.* New York: Random House, 1985.

O'Brien, Raymond J. *American Sublime: Landscape and Scenery of the Lower Hudson Valley.* New York: Columbia University Press, 1981.

Ringwald, Donald C. *Hudson River Day Line.* New York: Howell-North, 1965.

Sanchis, Frank E. *American Architecture: Westchester County, New York.* Croton-on-Hudson, N.Y.: North River Press, 1977.

Simpson, Jeffrey. *The Hudson River, 1850–1918: A Photographic Portrait.* Tarrytown, N.Y.: Sleepy Hollow Press, 1981.

——————————. *Officers and Gentlemen: Historic West Point in Photographs.* Tarrytown, N.Y.: Sleepy Hollow Press, 1982.

Tracy, Berry B. and Mary Black. *Federal Furniture and Decorative Arts at Boscobel.* New York: Harry N. Abrams, 1982.

Van Zandt, Roland. *Chronicles of the Hudson.* New Brunswick, N.J.: Rutgers University Press, 1971.

Zukowsky, John and Robbe Pierce Stimson. *Hudson River Villas.* New York: Rizzoli International Publications, 1985.

Index of Photographs

About the Photographer

Though **Ted Spiegel's** career in photojournalism keeps him constantly on the move throughout the world, the Hudson River Valley has been a continuous subject for his cameras over the course of a decade. His documentation of the cultural diversity and scenic richness of the region has been seen in a National Geographic Magazine article, a Scenic Hudson sponsored exhibit and Audio-Visual show *Humanity's River,* and a score of publications here and overseas. Mr. Spiegel's interest in the dual themes of environmental and historic preservation are reflected in his vision of the Valley as *An American Treasure.*

Mr. Spiegel's fascination with history has been seen in National Geographic Books such as *Isles of the Caribees, The Renaissance* and *The Vikings.* His environmental education has been enhanced by National Geographic articles on water, acid rain and biotechnology. His social reportages have included Rockefeller Foundation programs throughout the world. The book *Western Shores,* which he also wrote, spotlighted British Columbia's Pacific Coast; a recent volume, *American Ingenuity: The Ford Museum,* documents his abiding concern with the intimate details which visually convey place and time.

For Ted Spiegel, a book is "a printed invitation to the process of witnessing." In *An American Treasure,* Mr. Spiegel seeks to "encourage people to enjoy the pleasures and beauty of life in the Hudson River Valley."

Born in Newark, New Jersey, Ted Spiegel now makes his home in South Salem, New York—in the Hudson River Valley.

About the Author

Jeffrey Simpson's interest in photographic books was developed during his tenure as an assistant editor with the American Heritage Publishing Company and as an associate editor with Chanticleer Press. In books such as *The Way Life Was, The American Family, The Hudson River, 1850-1918,* and *Officers and Gentlemen* (the latter two published by Sleepy Hollow Press), Mr. Simpson has used the medium of photography to explore the social history of his subjects.

Presently the New York liaison for arts and antiques with *Architectural Digest,* Mr. Simpson has recently completed several architectural history reports, notably for the New York City Landmarks Commission and the Landmarks Society of Western New York State. Like Ted Spiegel, Jeffrey Simpson is concerned with history and preservation, themes which dominate both his written work and the exhibits for which he has served as curator.

Mr. Simpson currently resides in New York City, but has traveled extensively through the Hudson River Valley while preparing the text for *The Hudson River* and *An American Treasure.*

Acknowledgments

The assistance and cooperation of many people are necessary before a book such as *An American Treasure* reaches its readers. The editors, on behalf of the photographer and author, wish to express their appreciation to the numerous groups and individuals who helped make this book possible.

The Tourist Promotion Agencies of the Hudson River Valley counties provided lists of attractions, historic sites, and scenic points in their areas which helped the photographer in selecting the best subjects to shoot. Special thanks are due to the members of the Hudson River Valley Association and the Hudson River Study Project, whose thoughtful suggestions were of great value to us all. The cooperation of state and federal sites was essential, and greatly appreciated. And, to a large extent, *An American Treasure* would never have been completed had Jackson Hole Preserve, Inc. not been sympathetic to the book and its theme of preservation.

Project Editor: James Gullickson.
Design by Barry Eisenberg.
Maps by Edward J. McLaughlin.
Printed by Aristographics, Inc.
Binding by Bookbinders.